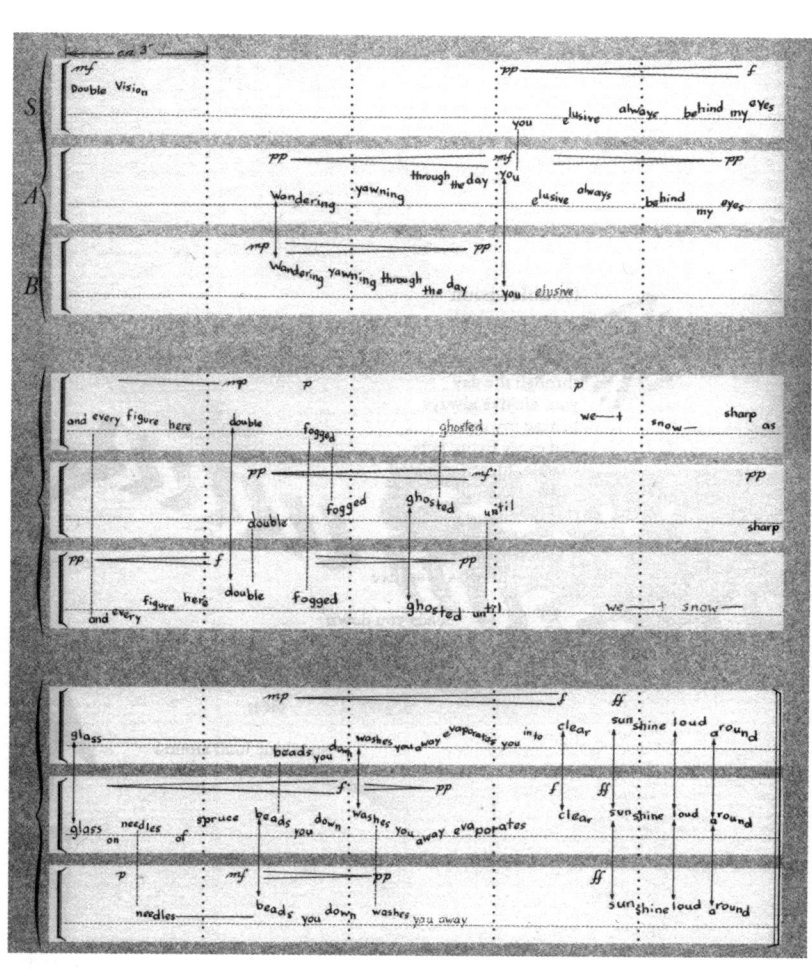

Paper Affair

Paper Affair

Poems Selected and New

Susan McMaster

Black Moss Press
2010

Copyright © 2010 Susan McMaster

Library and Archives Canada Cataloguing in Publication

McMaster, Susan
    Paper affair : poems selected and new / Susan McMaster.

Includes index.
ISBN 978-0-88753-468-3

    I. Title.

PS8575.M33P36 2010   C811'.54   C2010-900702-6

Cover design Marisa Wood

Endpapers "Double Vision", wordmusic for three speakers by Susan McMaster and Andrew McClure from *Pass this way again* (Underwhich, 1983)

Published by Black Moss Press at 2450 Byng Road, Windsor, Ontario, Canada, N8W 3E8. Black Moss books are distributed in Canada and the U.S. by LitDistCo. All orders should be directed there.

Black Moss would like to acknowledge the Canada Council for the Arts for its publishing program. Assistance was also provided by the Ontario Arts Council this year.

PRINTED IN CANADA

Dedicated to my father, Gordon McClure,
whose love of poetry seeded my own.

Contents

As the heart learns to pulse

lately, she remembers: **March**

Dark matter	14
Pandora	15
Bitter bread	17
The letter you do not send	18
The gardener's dream	19
The axion	20
Mail	21
Dangerous times	25
Fucking in the afternoon	26
Weekend friends	27
Lac Vert	28
The pleasure of lusting	29
Still enough	30
Out of the sleeping body dreams erupt	31
Postscript	32
Dismounting	33
The hummingbird	34
Real things	34
love is the word	35

lately, she remembers: **July**

How God sees	38
Perceiving a stable environment	39
The logic of hills	40
Outhouse	41
Beware	42
Starlings	43
The moth	44
one handful of bright feathers	45
It is my own sadness	45
Driving into night	46
Walking the Labyrinth – day 3: Benign	47

Ice	48
Certain days	49
Door	50
Ordinary: 1	51
Pray for me	52
Ordinary: 5	53
Old cedar	55

lately, she remembers: **November**

Supersymmetry	58
Hands in light	59
Beginnings	60
The naming	61
Birthday tales	62
All her soft angles	63
The old woman's chair	64
The old man's chair	64
Recycling	65
Prayers in space	66
Requiem for organ music	68
Ordinary: 7–8	69
The function of prayer	71
Spacetime quake	72
Ordinary: 10–12	73
The old couch	76
Yeast	77

lately, she remembers: **January**

Black locust fever	80
Choke	81
Scumbled	83
For my daughter, in hospital	84
For my daughter, coming home	85
Prayer for morning	85
At midnight talks fail: 1–5	86
Mont St-Hilaire	89
Daughter	90
dream strand: Falling	91

Red	92
my breath wasn't yours	93
Superstring	94
How dandelions prey	95
To admit the draw of starlight	96
The need of objects	97
How windows pray	98
Blame	99
Quantum world	100
Learning to ride	101
Today I turned everything around	102
World shift	103

So the mind learns to fly

Acknowledgments	107
Credits	108
Sources	109

*As the heart learns to pulse
to reason's sway
as the mind learns to follow
where the heart yearns to go*

lately, she remembers: **March**

Her palms are hungry. Oh, other parts too,
but in the night, now he's gone, and even the cat
finds elsewhere to sleep, it's her palms that ache
for the feel of his shoulder, right there in the centre
of her hand, where the bones come together, where
the flesh pillows, sparks at a careless touch. *The heart*
she calls it, to her, much more real than the erratic
muscle that lodges over her stomach,
stutters when she climbs the stairs too fast,
burns and knocks, a complaining roomer
always ready to whine.

> *In the rain-pattered night*
> *she rubs palms against the sheet,*
> *his hip – his shoulder –*
> *how they fit as he rolls*
> *onto his side, as she smoothes*
> *her hand down a muscled arm,*
> *slips it over his chest,*
> *circles, presses,*
> *tucks knees against thighs*
> *as she strokes*
> *further down, strokes the curl*
> *under the slow ribs,*
> *down the feathered belly,*
> *cups a soft rise.*

In the flat, empty bed, she covers her mouth,
brings a tongue into that crease –

cups her heart –
licks it dry.

Dark matter

To account for the motion of stars within galaxies and galaxies within clusters ... it is necessary to suppose ... the gravitational influence of much more mass than can be detected directly. Scientific American 252:5

The pull that holds us together
can't be explained just by our words,
by the things we do. What can account
for my wandering ellipse, your far-flung loop,
how we keep returning against all sense?
Baffled by light, I peer not at stars
but at dark distances between, see

streams of ancient particles pouring everywhere –
ghostly dimensions overlapping ours –
old lumpy debris scattered here and there –
burnt-out daydreams, ones about to form –

How much of the pull in our strange, quarky dance
comes from matter too tenuous to shine –

dark galaxies

Pandora

It was that one moment –
my hand on the jar in the morning kitchen,
the thumb edged with garden earth
rubbing its mound against the lid –

You all blame me.
You think I had a choice
to bring out the jar, or leave it locked
in the cupboard by the door till time had wound us
back to the start. You say I was careless,
or foolish, or wicked, or simply curious,
that sin you call *woman's*, as if men weren't the ones
always probing and prying and lifting up stones.

But you don't understand.
He'd gone out again, he who was sent
to be my companion, my lover, my joy.
Off to tend the flocks, or some such thing.
I'm afraid I didn't listen when he told me about it,
it all seemed too – oh predictable, so much
what he'd been ordered to do, as I had my chores
and no chance to question.

For they weren't *all* sealed away, hidden in that jar.
I didn't let them all out when I lifted the lid.
That joker – the one with the loud voice
living off that way, and so damned high up –
he gave us one to start with, *gratis*, free,
no effort on my part required to set it loose.

A simple sin, easy to ignore
for the longest time with all I had to do:
setting up the house, planting the garden,
discovering what those things were for,
his and mine, that fit so well
when we found out how.

Still, I felt it at times, behind my right ear
or underneath my breastbone,
at night when he was in the throes,

or after breakfast when the door had shut
and the dishes waited
and silence fell like a sheet.

That's when it ate at me:
first like a fly buzzing around, almost below notice;
then, a blackness that perched on my shoulder,
was always there; finally huge wings
that draped themselves over me
and took to smothering sight at the oddest times –
while I brushed my hair,
or listened to the rain –

boredom. That's all.
Such a small and simple sin
to topple a world.

And my right hand.
Four fingers. One thumb.
One hand that came to twitch and burn,
to clench in the night, jerk against a glass,
send it crashing to floor

And one day, when the sun shone in,
pulled me to the cupboard,
turned the cool key,
lifted out the jar –

What else could I have done?

Bitter bread

You prepare a feast of bitter bread,
of acid wine and rancid flesh,
then sit me down. *Now eat*, you hiss,
*Eat well of the wrongs that you did to me,
now chomp these chunks, now stuff them in!*

I will – I say – but not alone.
Pull up a chair. It's not only I
who must gorge till I'm sick,
till the rank meal's done.

For in love, you must know,
the meat of revenge
is the vengeful's bone,
the dregs of its wine
the avenger's sop.

And the bread that is thrust
on the one who has erred
in matters of love
must always be shared.

The letter you do not send

The letter
  you do not send
    grows until it blows against
      drags over my garden like
        torn sheets of newspaper
      uncovered in spring

                      words from the letter
                  you do not send
                tatter leaving dry branches

with the lies you tell
  about the letters
    you have not written
      season after season
        of discarded promises
          shredding into scraps
            of blurred dampening words
          blowing over my garden

                with the lies about the letters
                  you do not send
                  have not written
                  will not uncover
              this spring or any other season

years of letters unsent
            blowing
                  shredding
                        tearing apart

                into words I can no longer read
                and will no longer
                              say

The gardener's dream

I lay you on the bed
of grass
cut carefully with my sod knife
around your shape
with each of your
small cries
reach under, cut free
one sliver of turf
with its skein of root
its blade of grass
cut and place
it, a small green flame
on your uncovered skin
for each of your
sighs
lift, and plant
one more blade
one more green light
till round your form
the grass flames green
the earth below
freed blade by blade
of its cover, loosens
grows rich, grows warm
a bed hollowed deep
from your hollow cries

The last blade I place
with its crumble of soil
its gleaming leaf
on your still perfect forehead
then lift myself, lay
my gardener's tired body
on the mound of your greenly
flaming skin
press you, blanket you
between earth and sod
garden you in

The axion
Although light, axions would be abundant enough to account for the missing mass.

The anxious thought (two in the morning)
that this time the car went off the road,
the underlying (worse)
if only it did . . .

The nerve-wracking jiggle (knees under table)
as you race through your dinner,
the breath caught tight (in my throat)
as I watch . . .

The *Nothing*'s, the *Fine*'s,
the *Isn't it time*'s

we turned out the light? –
dissembled our fright . . .
burrowed into night . . .

anxieties drifting, pervading our hold,
chilling us colder than comfortless space –

this domestic place
smothering in the frigid, ungraspable grace of

I didn't want to hurt you . . .
You wouldn't want to know. . .

Mail

The mail carrier in the early dawn is writing
letters in her head: *I didn't say* – she snaps
the envelopes together with a rubber band,
leaves the station: *I didn't mean* –
Her letters always seem to start that way,
or maybe his do, she isn't sure.
Love is a tremulous business, she thinks,
an uncertain shaking between earth and sky.

She gets off the bus, heaves up her bag:
right side going, left coming back.
She tries to avoid it, but every job
carries its mark, its thirty-year hump;
she forgets to switch, loses track.
But there are good things too:
the rubber-soled thump of feet on the sidewalk,
each rolling down to press the earth
from heel to toe – no trembling here.

The mail carrier's man is a thousand miles away.
His letters are long: he wants to know
everything she thinks, each place she goes
from early rising to early bed.
But her days are sedate, her nights the same,
and so she writes. He's not convinced.
Sometimes she imagines him
running through her words over and over,
searching for proof of parties, orgies,
drunken embraces with drunken men.
He's right, in a way. What nights there were,
if any came like that, she'd keep to herself:
words on a page are too black, or white,
never quite fade.

There's Mrs. Jones, standing at her gate,
pulling up weeds, talking to the children,
waiting for the mail. This morning the mailwoman
has something to give, deals it out slowly
to make it seem more: a card from Liz –
'X marks the spot'; a telephone bill;

a SUPER SALE; and best saved for last,
a letter from Joe.

The mail carrier's man is an unemployed bum.
So her friends say: she's beginning to agree.
The government sent him for training (they paid),
but "I'm too old for that crap, and the girls are too young."
The carrier imagines a room in cool green,
white-shirted girls in feather-light shoes
looking out through glass at the Gatineau hills . . .
Then he headed west.

Her feet skirt a puddle, crackle through ice,
the first of the year. A rustle of leaves –
the lindens still glow though the maples are through.
She knows each tree on each block of her route,
when it buds, how it flowers. She knows each child,
each dog, each cat, how the Reverend died
shovelling snow last year; how his sisters now move
with frivolous steps in their faded old dresses,
giggle as they sweep away leaves from their path.
Is that how you feel with no man to answer to?

He says he's still dry. But some of his letters
don't make sense; the handwriting wanders.
He worked on a rig, but only for a week:
"It's dangerous," he wrote, "a man got killed."
She has to be fair: it's not his fault
there are no jobs left in the Golden West.
She thinks of him walking through dusty streets,
day after day, pounding along in his scuff-heeled Grebs,
steps in time with her regular tread.

Number 32 – locked as usual, curtains drawn.
She drops a circular in through the slot (flimsy, ugly thing).
A familiar creak: the old man's coming –
too bad just for that.

And now Miss Richards: "Good morning, lovely day!"
A nod, a smile, but Miss Richards keeps her distance,
never tries to pry. She's grateful for that.
Not that there's much to find out these days.

The familiar dreams have begun to fade.
The memory of her man – his smell, his touch –
doesn't have the power it used to have
to make her pulse like a violin's throat.

Mostly now she imagines him pacing,
pacing through the streets,
pacing through her words,
gathering rage, till he
slams into a bar,
scrawls a reply: HARRY'S
she reads on the placemat's edge,
or 24 HOUR GIRLS.

Nearing the end. Must be Jenny's birthday –
three parcels in the bag.
Then coffee at the corner, a chat with Georgette,
and home on the bus.
Why is he so angry? What has she done?

"Marry me," he'd said. "Get a job," she'd replied,
and, "I promise I'll write" –
but now he's the one who showers her with mail,
letters every day, two, even three,
now her hand trembles whenever she writes,
trying to find words grey enough
that they won't set him off.

At her own door, she pauses,
hunches her left shoulder against the empty bag,
slowly turns the key –

There it is, on the mat.

In spite of it all, the rages, the guilt,
in letters, he still has a peculiar sway
over her professional heart.
Maybe because she knows how old people
hover at windows, waiting for mail.
Maybe because *I love you* on a page seems
so much more real than any easy words.
How do other people tear letters up,

throw them away, leave them unanswered?
She can't imagine a letterless world.

She bends, picks it up,
holds it in her hand –
in her mind, sees the sisters
waving, smiling, as she passes empty-handed,
the two old, jubilant sisters
who don't seem to care
when she has nothing for them.

She slits the envelope with a practised thumb,
reads: "I've had enough."
reads: "I'm coming home."

Hardly dares hope . . .
No more letters for her to read?
No more words to tie her down?

Reads again. Grins.
No more waiting for the daily jolt?
Just flesh? Just man?
Just a *bum* of a man?

Laughs as she pulls a pen from her pocket,
laughs as she writes on her white front door
one last letter for him to read:

> PARCEL REFUSED.
> DAMAGED IN TRANSIT.
> DO NOT FORWARD.
> RETURN TO SENDER.

Steps inside. Locks it tight.
She's not waiting for the mail
anymore.

Dangerous times

It's one of those dangerous times
when everything seems too much to bear,
when everything you say, everything I do
grates on the other one,
turns us inside out with mad irritation.
Others have given up.
That's enough, they say, enough.
Let me go, let me be!
(let me go, let me be)
Such brilliant blooms they wave before my eyes –
young lovers, new lives –
while here we have a fading bouquet
of a few weedy flowers
(is it enough, let it be enough)

Fucking in the afternoon

Tempts the gods.

The baby's asleep, the child at school,
the plumber come and gone
(reminding us to clean our pumps).

We draw the curtains, lock the door,
pull off jeans and shirts, release
a whole day's muskiness
but
as scent welcomes warmth

the telephone rings.

He answers, I lie back, hopeful,
on the couch
but

the doorbell peals,
waking the baby,
who starts to cry
as down the street
the school bell rings
and Mother's on the phone
(if I have a minute) –

So
I take the receiver, open the curtains,
he pays the paperboy,
brings down the baby,
and

the last slight chance
of afternoon love
gone

we share instead
a cup of tea.

Weekend friends

When they leave, the lake
sharpens, clears
as if we'd turned the lens
on your father's binoculars,
hills step closer, water flashes in our faces
and we lie back, stare sleepily
at loons, the other shore.
"Alone at last," you say,
tipping your hat over your eyes,
but *together at last* is how it feels,
gathered into the bay
with the rocks and the pines
and crows *crak-crakking*
so much louder
than minutes before
when we called *Goodbye, goodbye*
to weekend friends.

Now we doze on the beach,
absorbed under a comforter of hazy clouds,
lulled by the whoosh and buzz of fly and wind.
Through half-closed lids you swing closer, recede
into the burn of sun from sand
    forward and back
        forward and back
            with the *loolooloo* of waves –

                    I surge, retreat,
               fall into dream,
            matching your dance
        with my own sleepy drift
  alone
    together
      at last and
            all one.

Lac Vert

The fog on the lake
so much like the press
of your skin on mine

a tender lie
of captured light
lyric unashamed

But metaphors like these
have been so often pulled
through poetry's eye

I hardly dare describe
except for you alone
the tremble of your skin

how it ripples like mine
under yours, under mine

how dusk and mist
blend water into sky
in a private poem

The pleasure of lusting

          – after you is to stroke,
with my finger, the hollow beside
your eye so lightly you only shift and turn
in your sleep – *hmm* – a small, satisfied sound
and your arm drops across me in sleepy
caress, and fits – under its weight
the arch leaves my back, I become
soft as the sheet, waver down
your snores

          – or to lie, blanket to chin
while you warm last night's coffee, lie
with one knee turned out, fingers idling
casual as the stroke for the cat who sometimes
rumbles beside us as we toss, feeling
everything become supple, fluid,
a watery terrain

          – and then to pull you
down to me, turn with one motion
from back to front, close my hands
around your ankles, close the triangle
as you rock me from below, as we
climb a long, slow wave to the
top, glide down

          – what pleasure, then
to drift into dream of rocking
together up wave after wave
or to wake, cup palm around
your shoulder while you doze
beside me, watching

          – two small, sleek blackbirds
            in the tree outside the window
                  whistle and preen –

                            roll again over you

Still enough

And yet returning
  in the night is still
    enough. I climb
      down from the plane
        into your soft quiet
          waves of talk drawing
          us into the shore, our
            skin lit like shadows of
              swimmers returning across
                sand into evening, your face
                  before bed a gleam drawing
                me into the dark soft
              sough of your breathing
              to rock against the surf of
              spare nighttime traffic, rock
             the stars warm as tea lights,
            blow the shadows through
           night into morning, your
          soft sighs returning on the
         surf of the dawn as we
        rock into light, still
      then, returning is yet
    still, enough
  enough
still.

Out of the sleeping body dreams erupt

And with this handful of dozing words
years later, adrift
on Lac Vert, lac rêve
where first your rhythms reached me
I feel tonight your ghost
slip kindly into mine
shrug me on like a coat
reach hands into my sleeves
sheath into my fingers
like gloves, I lean
back into your hold
as with a windy, companionable sigh
you slip my face like a mask
over your own damp dome
root your sweaty blond halo
in among my brown
crinkle my eyes with your grin
wriggle my hips
on this creaky wooden chair
settle your mismatched loins
into my creases
jerk out arms and legs
with a muscular joyful stretch
snap joints into place
tap my toes to your tune

        For one green beat
        I hear your music, with my ears

Postscript

This is the letter
you'll never receive,
I'll never send,
don't even write
in the hope that someday
you'll understand.

The life we live now
has an unshared shape.
You exist for me
to use – no longer you
who gives, withholds.

Mine is the story, and this
the last account.

All I need now
is a fictional you.
A paper affair.

Dismounting

When will I learn
how to dismount
with spring, grace,
in that moment of parting,
how not to fall
in a heap, or cling
to neck or mane
in a slipping embrace
that ends with a thump
on shaking knees

but swing smoothly down
as I've seen others do,
land light, square,
hand over the reins
to the next in line
with a casual nod,
walk smiling away,

No matter how rough
the ride, to let go
as if I don't care.

The hummingbird

This morning, the hummingbird
came back, for you,
hovered at the glass.
This afternoon, you brought me
a flower from the beach
a fuzzy-stemmed cinquefoil
not listed in the books.
You said, let's name it for us.
Our bird. Our private bloom.

Real things

    Let's talk about real things all this broody stuff
    is fine but whose turn is it to cook supper who
    tracked sand all over the floor who forgot to close
    the fridge door who gets to decide if we screw
    tonight and whose turn is it to say
                                             please

                                                             stay

◆

love is the word
for your brilliant flight
love your fall

death the word
for your fall
death your gleaming light

lately, she remembers: **July**

When the sky builds ladders
gold foil and cotton waste
heaps of creamy gray
lolling and soft

When blue pales then flares
silver strips gold
grey night settles
with a sigh on its side

You grow in me, roll
under my rolls
mound in my mounds
loosen, elide

And I climb from this tenor
whine of car
into slow bass Jacob
climb up ripples, rungs, folds

into your arms
to wrestle all through
the long dusky fall
from gold to night

wrestle with love
wrestle, subside

wrapped in sky

How God sees

The same way we
look out from top the
of the Gatineau Hills,
lean over the stone wall
at the Parkway's edge
and cover the whole expanse
of glittering green
in one wide sweep,
know, without tracking it,
how the river bends,
twists through fields
that lie like pillows
on their limestone bed,
how roads stitch between.

One glance, it's all there.

And then, pick a leaf
from the ivy on the wall,
cup it in your fingers,
trace the fine veins,
bend closer,
see

the whole wide valley
focus
in a green beam
along a slender rib –

ray out to the rim.

Perceiving a stable environment
Because the perceptual system compensates, our surroundings appear to be stable when we move.

The world sh ⁱ f ts as he moves through.
He approaches, it e x p a n d s,
passes, it tu
        r
    ,sn
nods, it   alt
      ters.

Elegant and precise are the compensations
for movements of the e
              y
          e,
for movements of
            the
                head,
                      for movements
  of the field,

        of the world as a whole:

     so adaptable is the universe to a

          self
         centered
          man.

The logic of hills

My ears are always popping here,
I yawn a lot, as if the air
were mountain air, too light and clear
to hold me down – amazing
the effect of a few days' quiet,
of a loon's manic whistle
on everyday gravity.

Pea soup tonight, and bread,
both homemade
on the low black stove.
You and the girls cook
while I finish up city work,
staring at the lake.

Now, the white-throat's evening tune –

Everything settles.
The logic of hills
repeated exactly
in the opal water
seems right, the way it is.

Could it possibly be
there's no more to know
than these lightheaded trees,
their perfect reflections –

Is it possible not to strive?

Outhouse

The only seat with a hole in it,
you name me *throne* for my power.
Built before the cabin's begun,
home to spiders and wasps
and shadowy bears in the night.
The one call no-one can ever refuse
no matter how late or dark.
All manner of daytime cover-ups
are exposed on my redolent heap,
many an indulgence paid for.
Oh you wriggle and squirm
at the thought of my eye
cocked at your bottom side.
But in my way, I'm discreet.
Dirt and disease are quickly cooked
by my rich bacterial tribe
into a useful soup.
And the trees grow a little taller,
the jack-in-the-pulpit thrives.

So deny me if you want to.
Set me back in the shadows,
grimace when you lift my lid.

But remember, along with philosophy
and politics and poetry,
you live to service me.

Mine is the lasting treasure
of all your bright songs and fine lies.

Beware

If you sit still on the rock
long enough, a child will come
to lean against you, stroke your cheek,
after a while, leave.
If you sit still on the rock long
enough, the cat arrives,
rubs against your back, your hand,
underneath your legs.
Insects, after a time,
seem to forget you're there,
look for noisier meals.
Crows squawk and fight,
swoop off over your head.

Your eyes, if you wait,
get used to the evening sun.
You start to see more clearly,
see the flat grasses, lit long and slanting,
turn green, translucent,
arrange themselves as paintings.
You discover bits of mica
glinting in small geodes
cracked open, full of splinters.

After a while, if you're still enough, long
enough, the rock begins
to rock, languorous, lapped,
the mesh under the water
made of yellow light
seems to lift you up.

Then the whole rock will tilt
if you're quiet,
very calm,
for a moment, become
                holes in air
                          humming wings
    (you, too
             cease to matter)

Starlings

(Outside my office window)   flocks of black starlings
                              fall
                                     from roof and chimney,
       cross flocks of white flakes
tossed
      side   – to mix
        ways   with the snow –
            from
                clouds   wind
     heavy   behind   up
                          head
            diagonals –
       own
    cut their
The birds
     swoop and   lift again
         land and
       from the crab trees
    and the banks
            of municipal rowan
            at the foot of the road
            that edges the cliff –

black
                                            hand-
                                               fuls
     confetti   of
               stars –
       wings –

thrown over trucks and sewers and bins –
                               (silent as paper)
                     (beyond the sealed glass)
                        (where I look in)

The moth

All night the moth beats across the pane
chasing the moon as we hurtle along the track.
I try to guide it out, but it fights my palms
hurtles, itself, backwards into black.

Then I notice, glistening on thumb's heel
powdered pearl – moth dust –

Moths escape webs by shedding scales
but one spider weaves a hanging tube
to guide the rush of the moth's frantic fall
till all powder shed, at the end it's trapped
by naked, ragged wings –

(your hands shine at the end of the day)
(your arms tunnel a headlong rush)

My hands in the train racket glisten with pearl.
The moth beats the window, frantic for the moon.

◆

    one handful of bright feathers
    shake
    fall
    and that is it
    done

◆

It is my own sadness
I must push through,
my own black weight
that shakes and tilts
on invisible wings,
my own wish to nest
in thistledown and silk
my own weak feet.
These birds are only birds,
not me, not you.
Whether they fight or fly,
nest or kill,
there are no stories here
but the ones I tell myself.

Driving into night

We are driving into real dark now,
no moon, a few fogged stars,.
The girls are asleep,
you're dozing, lulled –
when the cat starts to wail.

I answer, but at my voice
her cries grow suddenly loud,
so I hold out my hand,
make myself mute, calm
as the motor on the regular road,
as the smooth graded dimming
of sunset into night – it's all the same,
I tell her, here or anywhere,
it is all the same, we are asleep,
nothing at all to fear – and she pushes
against my hand, crawls onto my lap,
buries her face against a thigh,
presses, purrs – we are asleep, it is dark,
the bumps and turns and ruts
are only what always happens,
I am with you, I am present,
we are softly, heavily touching –

The lake smell.
The silence.

We are here.

Walking the labyrinth – day three: Benign

Sun! Yes! brisk hat, double coat, loop scarf, snippy boots, quick zipper ring *dum dum dum dum* snow snip ah air bones loose bounce round in all that unfooted wrinkle, *whee!* step step steady let jostle worries *time work enough enough* stitching shoulders up up sigh down up up breathe count– one two three hundred and sixteen steps to the middle – to the penny on the pile – to the student card flapping there, flipping off youth – turn to go, step one two and throat pours loose – *praise praise, all the hills, dona nobis peace, oh sun!* eyes open glisten gold over every pour blue on blue on blue –

                        wings wings behind my back

                                W

                                      w

       magpie *crak!*

   spits of light

chickadees squeak and eye me back

Ice

Where the river sluices under a sheen of ice
come weeks too early (months, years) –
what I still can't bear –
                      it knocks
me out the door
to the brink.

    Orange lamps
    from the opposite bank
    bar the black.

        Moonlight cuts.
        Far below, rapids hiss.

            Take one step forward –
                pillars rise – shafts of mist
                on the river's spine.

    One step back –
        they drop –
        no more than cracks in ice –

            forward –
back –
        forward –
            listen –

            who whispers there?
                (too late –
                    too soon)

            moonlight shifts
          (almost lips –
            almost arms)

      I step back –
  turn.

Glitter breaks
beneath my feet.

Certain days

On certain days I need the safety of packed small nodules of undemanding friends, thick stews, day-to-day talk, the soft hands and bobbing heads that beat around me, all warmer than my descending fever, all body heat of polyester shirts pressed between our white and well-fuzzed stomachs rolling their ways through food, drink, jokes, through hugs and cheek-brushing kisses practised over and over until noses no longer bump, eyelashes poke, or chins rasp ears, until the railing together of these smooth unintimate clasps is clamped, magnetic, firm.

On certain days I spend my energy spitting my cocoon and biting at it from inside. Then I have no tolerance for your flashes of magnesium brilliance, your clear naked barings of the world's undercorners, my own progenitive slime is still too translucent, the light shearing through still too sharp for my unshaped eyes. So show me no poetry, hide your bright paintings, melodic interior twists, keep your Pythagorean elbows to yourself!

Give me, instead, hamburgers, beer, a soft white belly,
a few pink hairs to fasten to mine –
then maybe –

if these last just long enough –
if these stay just thick enough –

> the white, micrometre wings can form fold dry
> and maybe –

>> something unconnected to you or me
>> to word or why

>>> can flop itself free, thrust out, fly

>>>> into god's
>>>> explosive
>>>> eye.

Door

When friends walk away too soon, you're left
in the draft from the November night blowing past
where they forgot to stand in the doorway, in their coats
and woolly hats, to say just one last thing and one
last thing more, while you shivered and laughed,
maybe wished they *would* go, because even in their shelter
the wind blows cold where you stand to see them off,
lean against the jamb in shirt and sock feet, rub elbows,
clutch arms, but even as they turn away at last,
you yourself add just one more word, one more
twist to the tale you can none of you seem
to let end – *wait* – press a bag into their hands –
for the long drive home, for lunch tomorrow –
till finally they say they really *must* –
and you wait while the car backs down the lane,
rounds the corner, before you flick off
the lights, lock the door, climb the stairs.
There'll be a mess in the morning,
proof you all let go, partying so well,
talking so loudly, it was hard to wind down
till you stood at the door shivering
and buzzing with spirits and words.

When a friend leaves too soon
the draft blows in.

Ordinary 1

Ordinary – *is it?*–
as bread
or the taste of water
    it is?
as the sky
shifting blue
to grey to
red
is silk
sheets, a satin coat,
a barge gold with bloom, she
should have it
for her decline, not this
tangled bed
damp
with her smell, its only
flowers
pilled on the sheets, it is pill
bottles by her side, an over-
stuffed locker – far too
tight
it is to enfold
        her
            how
                  she
    danced
                       it
      spangles
                        jet
                she
        swung
            is silk
  The ceiling lowers.

On the bedside table
is a glass of tepid
milk –
      ordinary . . .
            is it . . .
                  it shines.

Pray for me

Pray for me! – her fingers sharp as feather's spines
she clutched my hand. Her eyes were bare.
Of course, I replied, intending no more
than a gesture or two when the right time came
(her hands shook like birds in their delicate skin).
Pray for me . . . I heard it again as we raised
our glasses to her eighty years. I will, I said,
and turned away.

It's been years now since we laid her down
(her eyes cut through me into the cold),
folded her hands, closed her lids,
nested her under a blanket of snow.

But I find she creeps in. My nights aren't my own.
Her hands clutch mine, eyes open wide
if I try to sleep in an unpledged way.
I'm forced to pray, or her hands
and her bare, bare eyes
creep in.

Ordinary 5

Confronting it straight
this sunny afternoon,
    it is pear worm
    it is death date
fingers scaled with dirt
from under the hedge.
I pull out old plastic
and brittle Styrofoam.
Under the scraggle, periwinkle
glints. Blackbirds whistle
though the river floods
and ice-broken branches
cover the bank.

This spring my task is to
face it –
yet
    another friend –
far
    too soon.
        is it?
        your task?

Thistle, plantain, these I know,
lamb's ear, ragweed,
rough-leaved rose –

What use, all those years
of conversations shared
if words fail now?
        ordinary –
        is it . . .

I dredge through sun
on bits of snow,
trying to clear it,
      all day
            all day

         free
a patch of order
in the scatter of gravel, litter, roots.
Is there a way
to green
    it
      this black?

The few weeds I know
yield to my pull.

Old cedar

Old cedar, bent
into a welcoming seat
far back in the woods
where no-one goes
you domesticate this carpet
of rattling leaves
hang lights on the branches
everywhere for me
sound the last call
of a departing loon
music for my doze
tall, quiet tree
I stretch along your length
face-down, hands dangle
under your arch
cheek presses moss
breasts and knees clasp
your muscular smooth rise
as the last pale
flies of a fading year
brush past the lids
I lower to see
the walls of your home
rise everywhere, glow
slower –
       slow –
              sleep –
                     a cell
                            in your mind.

lately, she remembers: **November**

Today, she controls the post. Man, he used to keep her
hanging letter by letter on the daily mail – long-distance
suspense, delayed delivery – of what she once
mistook for love. This is the shade that stood between
her and her days, ate them up.

> *You're wrong. You don't remember.*
> *He really loved me.*

> And you know this – how? – from letters
> scrawled in bars?

She lifts a few cards from the dripping box. Slams the
door on pelt and thud.

> It was a dark back road. No-one knew where you
> were. No-one expected you home.

> *He never hurt me before.*

> It was a dark back road. No-one knew where you were.

> *No-one expected me home . . .*

The piano, its mathematics of blond clear notes in the
sun-flooded air. Scales and chords and songs fall down
in dusty blocks. Today, this harmony fills quiet mornings
better than straining for the postman's step.

> *For years those notes eluded my touch . . .*

> The storm-tossed lake . . .

> *The next day, I swam and dove through waves,*
> *floating over rocks, resting on the swell.*

> Soft clear notes of rippling sun, water like jade.

> *All alone. Post that man.*

Still, she always looks –

Supersymmetry
Supersymmetry . . . relates every known particle to a partner that has a different spin and much greater mass.

To every gesture of yours I see
to every word you hear
is bound a weight much greater
that hangs in darker air

is bound a shade that mimics light
with faithless symmetry
distorts embraces, blackens words
clouds all clarity

For all I see when I watch you now
is the shadow side of the glow
and from your face it's easy to tell
how you weight my words, how you know

that partnered to giving is turning away
that desire brings desire to deny, betray
that love can defeat its own bright force
with its own bitter symmetry

Hands in light

Hands in light, my belly rounding
under laxing sun, sun spreading
its ripples under the water,
criss-crossed, knotted,
waving on the sandy bottom
like the nets they were weaving
that summer on the shore,
so fine that when we walked away
they seemed to be holding nothing.

Sand – net – water –
the wind – on your skin
where the rash of poison ivy
may show in a day or two.
You were trying to dig it out,
but it keeps coming back,
as regular, returning,
as the nets under the water
that lie on my feet,
lace them with questions
of knotting, dissolving,
of shifting sand under,
between sole and toes.

We are wrong to imagine
we can escape the blisters and itch
simply by wishing.

As wrong to imagine
we can pull these ripples tight,
knot this fluid net
into a rigid pattern,

predict what any mesh
will hold on to
or let go.

Beginnings

How can all this –
all these large
children, insurance plans,
roof repairs, weekends
at the lake – have sprung
from a few simple choices
made so young?
Progenitor, not I!
An ant, or a bee
or a piston in a car –
one part of a whole
just doing my part,
and God, if there is one,
warp to our woof,
screen to our image,
eyes for our show,
no more the Beginning
than we are the End –
etcetera – p.s. –
beginning
again . . .

The naming
for Aven

I walked through mountains
once, in my sleep
there were avens
everywhere
springing from grit and shale
a kestrel wheeling
a pica's whistle
and so far I could hardly hear it
a horned lark's cry

Or was it you, calling out
with the high wild wind
calling out your name
spiralling mare's tails
across the thin sky
rustling the low stars
clustered at my feet

Surely it was you
in the white rush of water
cascading in a blue tumult
towards me from the peaks

exultant over stone

Birthday tales

They were living, she tells me, beside a ravine –
one room upstairs. They tied strings across the ceiling,
strings and strings again, overlapping them into
a lattice of shadows, a web to hang their lives from –
lights, mobiles, clothes, and finally my cradle.

She won't say much about the birth,
about pain that racked the bones of her back
till they blanked her with gas – white shadows descending
from a thick black ceiling – though she'll tell me how
he pushed past nurses, was only stopped
by that last, locked door.

She doesn't describe the first teating,
how that toothless small mouth grabbed
with surprising bone at transparent skin
which reddened, cracked, finally yielded
to the rhythmic, gentle draining, the water of sound,
shows me instead the photos he took
through the glass, the card from my wrist
he pasted beside them.

Now, on my birthday, if I want to know,
she'll tell me again of the room, cradle, photos,
all she now remembers, what she chooses now to know.

As I, today, tell stories for my daughters,
but also for her, of the cramping,
the tearing, the suckling, the cries,
the man beside the birthing bed,
teeth marks on his hand –

And then we'll both recall
how they held our daughters out to us,

placed them in our arms
like chrysanthemums.

All her soft angles

The bony angles of a mother's thin knee,
questions her husband can't answer,
ones she won't ask,
delays of children reaching for bed-time
ride-abouts, knockabouts, dangerous tales,
stockings which seldom tear but always
pull over empty space,
the pulse of her elbow,
questions that, answered, find their way
to the heart again,
the soft swirl of veins broken, submerged
into gaps between bones,
the fat delves of perfume
for a child's blunt nose.

In mother's inner spaces, all her soft folds
are answers, questions, angles unnoticed
by all but her. Hidden replies.

The old woman's chair

It's the holding on to
I envy, the springing back
so softly from every press
without a flinch or groan,
I want to sink into her creases
with the other dust and grime,
hide my flesh in her grooves,
let my stuffing hang out
under cat-scratched arms,
exude a human sigh
as you settle into my lap.
I want to stay around for years,
too useful to discard,
too heartless to care –
outlive you every one!

The old man's chair

My lap yearns for your heat,
arms curve to reach you,
rigid joints relax
only when your humidities
fill the air around me,
sink damply into my fabric,
grease my back with sweat and oil.
When at last your jittering heels
have rubbed away my sheen,
flattened my nap,
scrubbed through to my supports –
then – shabby, creaking,
I am finally fulfilled –
embodied, I gleam.

Recycling

When I was young I gave all my secrets to you, spilling over
in great armfuls, messy slops of unmanageable entrails, rags
and boxes, piles and tail-ends of rolling milling bits that kept
tumbling from my fingers worse than handfuls and handfuls
of marbles – *here*, I said, *here*, I can't contain these any more,
my bags are stuffed and splitting, the zippers completely shot.
I have no cupboards with doors that close, they're stuck in
their guides, gummed up with leftovers, my drawers jam
open, scatter underwear torn and stained – *help me*, I said, I
can't hold on, please take me in hand, clean and sweep and
dump or at least pile away all my messy leavings on your own
ordered shelves –

And you rolled up your sleeves –

So why this residue? Twenty years later,
the secrets you swept up, dumped into the trash,
like bleach and old paint keep seeping back,
the anger you burned still hangs in the air,
opens blisters inside if we breathe too deep.

Now it's you who sits slumped, hands spread wide –
Your turn, you say, *your job this time* –

Time for finer siftings
to separate simple rot
from what will always cut,
time to grind up, melt down, discard
the useless at last.

Time to make room – my turn
to make room for you.

Prayers in space

Voyager 2 zoomed past the ringed planet Neptune and its icy moon Triton early this morning, beaming back strange and spectacular photographs. Ottawa Citizen, 15 March 1989

In the paper all week
photographs, reports
from a world we've never seen
as I waited for you to die
tossed, restless, dreaming
waking from dreams
shadowed, unremembered
full of alien forms
your curious eyes
tracing far signs
light years away
the connection between
what you saw and
we received
heard from your sendings
more and more tenuous
more and more stretched

The images returned this morning revealed a world unlike any we've ever seen.

Fainter your words, as the week drew on
fainter the descriptions
of unexplored reaches
though still we could vaguely see
with streaming eyes
what was filling your sight –
volcanoes of ice
crystals exploding skyward
gorgeous in blue

Until its official "near encounter" period ends, Voyager 2 will look back over its shoulder at Neptune. Then it will head toward interstellar space.

And still I kept hoping
still couldn't believe
you would actually go
even as we sat
together in the garden
one night while you lay drifting
still linked
still holding
but farther and farther
sat talking of you
watching the moon
subsume in earth's shadow
round out
glow

Now Voyager 2 is leaving not only the planet Neptune, but this solar system . . .

For a few days more
you sent us visions
from the very edge

then, this morning
stepped off the last orbit
that might have brought you back
curved away alone
into the gleaming dark

     plunged behind the stars

Requiem for organ music

beep dye me right through
        with your bumptious
              words spindle in
                    through my ears fill my throat
              heat and swingle
    up through my souls
             with your willing absurds
                            seep out
      from my loins organs dance
      to your tunes body note
                                  cells eat
        syls and labials
              hair net and twine and catch
            beep juices
                  (hhh-arts breadth)

                                O

                        rend-

                er me able
        to breathe

  (your death)

Ordinary

7

She lies so still I can hardly tell
if she's here or gone
>   *why is it, when it strikes*
>   *so many, do I still stand*
but for the morphine
rasp of her breath.
"No!" she shouts, "No!"
and rattles in her tubes,
her punctured hand
searching blind for the sheet
to rub it, to rub

it – she opens
her eyes –
>   *it is*
>   claw
>   thud
>   *it is*
>   a baffled
>   fog.

>   "The button," she croaks
around the tube in her throat.

>   I move
>   too fast, hit the bed, knock it,
>   jar the needle, pump
>   the drug, pump
>   it, pump it
in.

"It's okay now," she whispers,
"It's okay."

I brace against the wall.
Try to smile back.

8

It is one of the other days,
the ones when
> *she lies so still I can hardly tell*
> *if she's here or gone*
I just want to forget it,
when a nap on the couch
seems all I can handle,
when an unpaid bill
feels more urgent
than it is.
> *Oh god, not the phone!*
I slap down my book, rise
only because
I can't bear to think
I'll miss it – the last words –
> "hold me up, make me whole" –
words she never says at all.

"Is it a good time to call?
How are *you* today?"
Her voice.
> It's light.

The function of prayer

Thunder, and the wind at my back from a storm
that passes by the granite shelf dropped
by ancient ice on an unnamed hummock
in the river's long drench
maybe also for this –
                        to cup our fire
of pine cones and bark, form a ledge
for the tea of sweet gale simmering
in a blue tin pot, hold us steady
against the lap of black and pewter
waves that glint at our feet –

    pause –

receive.

Spacetime quake
Tremors in the structure of spacetime . . . so small there is only indirect evidence for their existence.

Who doesn't carry private darkness
shadows in the night
that shake the definitions
quiver them into doubt

who doesn't sometimes shiver, quake
with memory, loss
for a moment, lose track
of the matter at hand

drift away from the forces
that bind us into place
on predictable courses

ache toward the space
(the bright, imagined space)
where darkness
streams light

Ordinary

10

Terror of it can't last
every minute of the day.
  and it wakes me
  sobbing, wakes me
Glands wear out
before bodies do.
Look –
  raspberries ripening by the road –
    wild green plums deepening to blue –
      listen – a thrush carolling far
       back in the woods.

The sun goes down.
  It is a rainbow –
      swirl –
    to medicated
        eyes –
     a flurry –
    a deer –
   it steps
    through.

11

We can only endure it.
The dread, the sweats,
  terror of it can't last
  every minute of the day
as it shrinks off flesh.
Endure the watch.
Brace the walls
as a last stray beam
gilds her bed.

It is too late.
There's no time left
for rage or fear.

                    The doctor arrives.
I straighten the sheet,
remove the untouched milk, the tray.
Close the door
on it.
                    Walk through jet
            spangled with stars
                            to the river's edge.

12

It comes.
The call.
            we can only endure it
            the dread, the sweats
I climb up the hill
to the Rideau Falls
it buzzes
from the phone
to my feet
I buzz
lean over
the plunge
feel *it is*
cold
cannot speak *it*
I can not
speak
listen to
it the sounds
that come out
of my throat
as I fall
down
it
fall
eyes stream
it
hands
clutch
at *it* the

iron
fence
I do not know
how to
turn *it*
cannot find
air
enough to
stand in
it cannot
stand
it
or walk
it
blasted
with spray *it*
pounds
it
drenches
it
will not
stop
will not
let me
hear her
it will
not let
me pull her
back
from *it*
the slam of
it
I can
not turn
away from
it
she
falls and
      falls
           mouth full
                  of roar

The old couch

Still half-whole, most of a back,
two legs, a frame, a tattered seat.
Surely some glue and care could flatter
these bits together for another year.
But would I last, you ask, would I hold?
And it's true I was never more than ash
stained to mimic mahogany,
machined instead of carved,
acetate passing for silk.
My joints were never tight enough
to offer a safe support – O, I was
shifty and complaining
from the first, fresh-bought day!
But I fooled you for awhile
because you wanted me to.
You gloried in my presumption,
showed me off to your friends,
wore me out with parties,
decked in scarlet and green.
You rocked in my arms
to the beat of guitars,
spilled chilli and beer on my knees.
You cracked my shins with use.

The parties have come to an end,
it seems, the red is lady grey,
and you have no room in your cellars now
for the cracked, the old, the sham.
So toss me into the flames
if kindling is all you see.
Lie back and bask on your oak divan
and I'll toast you one more time
in the heat of a flagrant past!

Yeast

This is for all
the things we start on,
hold like a ball of
unrisen dough
warm in our hands,
imagine the loaf
risen, baked,
glazed and golden,
sitting there on the table
ready to share
with others drawn
to the sweet, yeasty smell
of two friends succeeding
in putting away
against tomorrow's hunger – one
sunny afternoon, two women
who pause
to stir together
the plain, ancient mix
of water, and grain

then draw from the air
where it always waits
the yeast, to join
with our kneading hands
to make this live –

this loaf we see so clearly
waiting to rise.

lately, she remembers: **January**

Look, he said – branches inked against the snow
bring it back – his voice – held in the trees,
as he called her to see the delicate spread.
They bought the lot, raised the walls,
and still the cabin, though slanted, stands.
But no-one can really claim the woods.
Thirty years of cutting brush, clearing paths,
pulling stones, marked the ground hardly at all.
Lake and shore took step and stroke,
washed them away. Rocks on the beach
caught their fires in rings of smoke,
but tumbled aside each winter with the ice.

Yet, somehow, the trees seemed their own.
The yellow birch beyond the door
layered bark with children's growth.
Two tall spruces hid the walls from boaters' eyes.
Oaks bronzed their seasons, summer to fall.
Maples and aspens blanketed the roof in red and gold.
Pines and cedars greeted them each year
						with evergreen.

Black locust fever

There are children in the locust crown,
hanging sprays of twigs and leaves

turned legs and arms that twist and tap
sundown along the horizontal stage

of uncut plank, of thicker branch.
A rustling applause hisses above

the surge of highway, frog croak and slam
of starting car beyond the second-

story glass where all together meet –
my legs and arms that quiver, reflect

the leafy curl of the children's step
in the dusky pane, my eyes that lift

to follow their clap, my blink, their bow –
before the storm sweeps downtown,

leaves us to dance unheeded, alone –
the children and I in the locust crown.

Choke

Sitting here in the driver's seat
with still your library card, insurance forms, bills,
underneath the dash, cracked seat cracking
even more every day, under me as under you –
I want to explain –

Your widow gave the car to your son, not me,
but his legs were too long to cram behind the wheel,
he didn't like the engine, noisy and small,
passed it on to me, with the choke you worried about
as you lay in your hospital bed, afraid we wouldn't know
how to handle it right.

As I worry too, lending it now to your daughter or mine,
push the choke back in when they return with it still out
and flooding the motor with a mixture too rich
and billowing beyond the tidy confines
of the metal hood.

All your life, you woke up choking, dreaming of an umbrella
shoved down your throat, a strange uneasy symbol – for what?
– you never said, and no-one's asked your wife – choking
herself at unexpected moments still on the waste of your loss,
on billows of smoke staining fingers, teeth, lungs, coating the
windshield with a greasy film.

"Buy a hundred umbrellas for a dollar," you used to say,
"sell them for two." And "This car has to last me
till the day I die."

I've emptied the ashtray, try once in a while to tidy the rest,
still guard your packages of tools, plugs, fan belt,
wires to jump the charge from your car to your son's
when the mercury falls below the damp bite
of your childhood home on the Devon coast
where the fog billowed in so bitter and chill
in your memories and tales, you could never
quite believe in a cold worse than that, an inland cold,
harsh enough to freeze wheels solid in their ruts,
kill any engine's spark.

At the end, you saw butterflies
fluttering on the walls,
butterflies, and your face
when the movement left it,
yellow, carved,
hair a white halo
on an anti-religious skull.
Agnostic to the last,
you left no messages,
made no pleas,
tolerated us there
as you always had,
let us continue each in turn
to hold your hand,
to sit beside you,
no way to convey
what you saw through the haze,
what final faint sounds
you heard as the mechanism
seized – coughed –
stopped.

Now I voyage back and forth on my own small circuits,
follow the instructions in the manual you thumbed,
tune and fuel the engine according to your schedule,
rearrange the tools, leaf your maps in with mine,
hold and release the choke by the sound of a motor
I know nothing about.

Hearing your voice.
Hoping I'm doing it right.
Hoping it's what you wanted.
Holding, and releasing,
like your hand,
at the end.

Scumbled

My life has become so thick that it has no
clear spots now for even a line of five or a dozen
words without practical intent. No single corner
in this burgeoning scramble is left to tend a useless
thought among the jumble of nourishing grains,
solid roots, and aggressive beans I weed and hoe
for so many needs.

Yet still I taste them – words – a handful –
the fresh savour of berries I'd plant if ever
I had time to notice their absence, a moment
to remember that the fruits of another's digging,
no matter how sweet, are not my own.

Oh, I know any crop raised in this northern
clime might be sour, too meagre for use –
such long dark winters, freezing rains.

Still, surely a few could be carefully seeded
at the cultivated edge of the useful plants –

        scumbled among the sweet gale fronds
where the weeds begin.

For my daughter, in hospital

Laugh in the face of the devil!
Laugh in the face of death!
Those who crouch and tremble
succumb to loss and theft
of all they hold most closely,
all they hold most near.

Sing in the mouth of the monster!
Dance in the arms of fear!
Nothing can break this fever
but love to rage and sear
through ice to icy courage,
through panic to panic strength

> – in the darkness, a space
> a quiet space
> that globes a quiet flame
> in the roaring storm
> a word
> under the roar of pain –

All I can give is all I have.
Child, all I have is yours.

> – in the hands of the air
> in the rock of the earth
> in the whisper and ease of night –

> in your hands, oh Lord, I beg thee –

> carry my child to light.

For my daughter, coming home

all is blue
sky sings
and I

Prayer
for a morning
not yet frayed
for every mourning
night endured
that wakes to ease
in the breathing chest
warmth of joints
taste of rest
shake out
the sky
blue silk
of day

At midnight, talks fail

1

And here we are: herded into a ragged string
burdened with signs, wrapped in scarves
against sunrise cold. They chivvy at our heels,
bark us into motion – colleagues, familiar
from a morning *hello*, are suddenly strange,
imbued with command. I thought they were sheep
like the rest of us shufflers, but, heated by conflict,
they've shrugged off wool, become dogs or mules
who snap at intruders, nip us into strength.

And we, are we still sheep for the shearing?
I glance at the tower where I stabled for so long,
at the stall where I nosed and snuffled for hours
clocked by the tick in a well-lit box.
Beside me, my fellows lift their heads
to scan the horizon, breathe the air.
Cut off from feed, barred from warmth,
we've pulled on coats over shorn shoulders,
jumped the fence. Here, on the loose,
the sky is our cover, legs our heat.

The wind grabs my sign.

I leap to hold on, leap like a goat
kicking its heels
at the arc of the sun.

2

When clouds drift over
We pull on hats and gloves,
reach for the warmth
of coffee and muffins brought
by the arriving members
of our restless herd.

Their turn now
to tread the hours.
Beside us, they also
pause to feed
before pulling on jackets,
shouldering signs,
readying their tack
to take their places
in the roofless round.
Deepen our steps.

3

An indoor huncher, he closed his blinds
to pinpricking light, passed me by
with a preoccupied nod when we shared a hall.
Now thrust outside every day at dawn
to tromp the lines under a blaze that burns
pale skin to boiling, polishes brown
to an angry sheen, he's tramping, not pecking.
It's feet now, not fingers, that tap
and tap through promised hours —

But not alone. Here, in the open,
dusted with grime, enamelled by sun,
scraped by wind, this friend discovered
on the strikers' march, shares
my worries, offers his own. We trudge
in tandem through daily thickets
of children, money, movies, books.

On the baking curb, his shadow and mine
blend into one.

4

And still we walk
The red that flared
over our heads

sinks into night,
then morning again
till we live in its turn,
mark our round
by its darkening measure.
After so many weeks,
now months, on the line,
we draw in breath
through the weather's weave,
exhaled from the pavement,
bushes, trees,
from wind devils sweeping
up against the walls
that bind us close –
as an empty hearth
holds to its stones
the hungry and cold.

Mont St-Hilaire
for Quatre-vingts

It's your scramble
that brought me up here,
your willing heave
to this scarp,
where you munch,
as pleased by the alpine
meadow grass
as I am by the blue
and ochre haze
of farmer's fields
below my feet,
the flute of thrush
in the woods behind,
the slanted light
through flaming leaves
and friends
who share
this autumn ride
up such a rocky slope
into this dream –

Where I stand on a mountain
while you graze by my side,
feel the world reel away
like lead on a line.

Daughter

And then to know
how to leave it all behind,
give it all up
when talent and luck
have reached their end,
when aging muscles
no longer respond
to a slowing brain,
to let go at last
and stand here now,
blocked at the gate,
watching the girl
who with fourteen skinny years
can float and drive and lift
her mount and herself
beyond any grace
I could hope to approach.

*Beware the selfish beast
in the old woman's breast,
beware her stubborn dream
of a different fate.*

dream strand: Falling

I'm afraid through the tumble
of dreams their shifting air
flinging corners doors stairs
rough metal gates braced to toss
me onto my flailing self
again the steps are suddenly
steep before me I am
falling down breaking
stick wood splintering down
the slope white before me
curved like a hook at the end
catching tumbling me hard
into the rasping wall that comes
up *crack* into my cheek smashes
fractures shoulder glass
breaking the mind *crashing* down
these stairs and I turn
my back and *cling*

Red

Death is not red
in the cancer ward.
The vibrant red ivy
I bring you for fall
shrinks under fluorescence
into a bit of old tat
mistakenly dropped –
no rain or blue wind
carried in on the leaves
I prop in dry glass
knocked aside
by the friend
who bends over your bed
to catch
the last mutter
dry words
from dry lips

My handful of sun
rustles to the floor
rustles behind
as you pass
you pass

pass through
you pass

◆

my breath wasn't yours
to take away
my heart's beat
wasn't yours to
deny
give me back my
swallows they're
mine that's my saliva
filling my throat
that's my salt
fluid pouring over
cheeks mouth eyes
pouring over
it's my libation
I can I can I will
I will breathe
I will cry for you
I will if I wish
I will cry

Superstring
Superstring theory ... ascribes as many as 11 dimensions to spacetime.

Each year more uncoverings –

what we might do
if only we cared,
where we might go,
who we might be
if only we dared
to opt for another
universe –

                    coincident, invisible
                    possibilities

How dandelions prey

Keep stamping me out!
Keep cutting and burning
and digging me up,
root stem and head.
Work at it, buddy!
Your obsessive attacks
just clear away the riff-raff –
plantain, ragweed,
crabgrass, vetch –
undisciplined louts
who grow any which way
without purpose or plan,
who straggle and sprawl
in showy display,
never notice or care
as they callously smother
my fecund broadcast,
my airy thistles of uplift,
my disseminate spread –

For I have a goal – to cover each
inch with my own bright shower,
strangle all competitors
with jagged nailed fingers,
convert every garden
to *Dandelion*.

So weed me like crazy!
Clear the way – clear the way.
Give me one lax moment
in a perfectly trimmed world –
and you all be under my sway.

To admit the draw of starlight

To admit the draw of starlight
how the world breaks in pieces
around me all the time

how time breaks in fragments
air lifts and shatters
sidewalks crack and fall

To admit the draw
of your entropic eyes
the way trees shift in their quarters of sky

the way ice corrugates in spring
and how its sheen can't be even briefly held
on eye's hot sheer

To admit your kiss
the shattering dark and fall
of bright pieces over under through me
how the world bursts and shakes around me all the time

At the water's edge
crayfish
bared in the spring mud

their claws
their fishy smell

The need of objects

The need of objects to be used
their longing to embrace
our momentary soft shadows
in plastic and metal arms
as the window on the stairway
beckons through dust
glass clears before my eyes
to hold up the view
like a photograph, or prism
draw me deeper into the embrasure
perhaps the first to stand here
in all the dozen years
since the building was raised,
on a spot of floor unmarked
by scuffing feet, lean my hands
on an unworn sill
one solitary third-floor window
with tree, and stone wall
behind a screen of rain

> *come closer*
> *look through*

How windows pray

You took
me by surprise
appearing that way so
suddenly
in the frame
small, below me, far
too far to speak
to or greet
glassed off
in any case
you wore
lightness, I remember
cream your clothes
and pale your hair
a sturdy figure
stepping lightly
into view, gesturing
at someone I
couldn't see
turned away
but o!
the lightness
when I saw you there
in me

Blame

So you want me to explain, do you,
list my complaints.
What do you want to know?
How I push through newspapers, candy wrappers,
schoolbags, on the living room floor,
how I feel when I'm driving alone
with the radio going full blast,
how I can't grab a thing to hold on to,
don't even know what I want.
except that it's something else?
Would it help if you heard the list
of my blessings and how I count them
over and over?
Could you believe me if I said the problem
is, there's nothing wrong,
no-one to blame, to point to
and say, *that's where it comes from,
this despair*.

That the worst thing is,
it's not your fault.

Quantum world
In an infinite quantum future, anything that can happen, eventually will.

If you have trouble holding on,
if you can't understand
why things are exactly
as they appear or else
never that at all

then it makes perfect sense
that the whole fine structure
could dissolve at whim
something come from nothing
be here, there, or nowhere

and a heart that beats or dies
without known cause
is reason
breaking
free

Learning to ride

Before I entered this curious new world
of body direct, it was naming alone
that stood for all else, the flap
of the tongue, labile and strong,
the only muscular motion
I'd learned to control.
Held thus, at tongue's length,
the world made sense,
a black and white tale patterned
in words I could stand back to read.

Tear them up, pull them away,
rip them into tendrils coiling
underfoot – and find –

A steady pulsing region
of thick grounded motion,
a shadowed wild land
of caverns, valleys,
always changing footing,
where I move like a tracker,
like a cat, like a deer,
to the beat of tissues,
flex of sinews,
spring of limbs,
loose, aware,
learning to learn
a whole new language
of heat and sweat,
push and groan,
learning to discard
the ancient metaphors
of love and soul and existential pain
for the uncoded strophes
of pulse and breath.

Learning to ride
the muscular heart,
the solid bone.

Today I turned everything around

I turned the flowers
to nod to the wall,
spiny backs exposed,
flipped the painting,
uncovered a tear
where the framing knife slipped,
swivelled the armchair,
found cloth torn by cats
on the padded back,
up-ended the tables,
reversed the rug,
split the walls open to the studs,
pulled out insulation,
ripped up floorboards,
yanked through nails,
reached into sewers,
wrenched them inside out,
tore the house away
from power lines, its web of pipes,
shook out furniture,
knocked off sod and trees,
flipped the roof,
punched out the cellar,
crushed the shell
into a ball,
and held it over your head –

You looked up
as I looked down –

you were so
small.

World shift

What a strange and lovely place.
Seen through this lens our house by the river
sparkles and gleams,
birds eat from our hands,
chrysanthemums and tulips flower into trees

But the oddest thing
is how time can half-step
back on itself,
can sometimes be
at the call of dreams,
on command, rewind
replay for our pleasure our happiest days

So close it sometimes seems –
this other space –

just one impossible step
backwards and away.

*So the mind learns to fly
to match the heart's leap
so the heart soars at last
across the mind's divide*

Acknowledgments

Paper Affair presents poems starting with the publication of my first solo poetry collection in 1986, and including new uncollected pieces up to 2009. It does not cover my wordmusic or performance works with First Draft, SugarBeat, and Geode Music & Poetry.

The selection and arrangement of the poems owes a great deal to the creative editing of a board including Keesha Bellemore, Kellie Chouinard, Courtney Deluzio, Jessica Dennis, Jordenne Rachelle, Erica Di Maio, Linh Giang, Rachel Kovach, Micheal Laverty, Erin Lukas, Jenn McMullian, Courtney Steel, Marie Veltri, and Marisa Wood. It also owes much to Betsy Struthers, Renate Mohr, Lynn Miles, Joanne Proulx, and Mary Borsky. I would particularly like to express my gratitude to Black Moss publisher Marty Gervais for his committed interest in my work, his generous and warm support, and his clear editorial eye. Thanks to Marisa Wood for the cover, the crew for a lovely book design and to Karen Monck for shepherding it through.

My father, Gordon McClure, was my first mentor, sharing his deep love of poetry with me from my early childhood. Crucial to my later development were bpNichol, George Johnston, Elizabeth Brewster, Doug Barbour, Christopher Levenson, Miriam Waddington, and Fred Wah. Among writing friends, Ronnie R. Brown, Blaine Marchand, Colin Morton, Carolyn Smart, Betsy Struthers, and Bronwen Wallace, have been central. I would like to express my deep appreciation to publishers Colin Morton and Mary Lee Bragg of Ouroboros, Alex Inglis of Balmuir, Bob Hilderley and Susan Hannah of Quarry, John Flood of Penumbra, Ada Donati and Giorgio Stefani of Schifanoia Editore, Penn Kemp and Gavin Carstairs of Pendas Productions, bpNichol of Underwhich Editions, and the League of Canadian Poets. Without the constant support of my community, friends, and family, especially, Betty, Ian, Aven, Morel, and Gwen, this book would never have appeared.

Not least, I would like to thank the Canada Council for the Arts, the Ontario Arts Council, the Regional Municipality of Ottawa-Carleton, the City of Ottawa, and the Writer's Trust, for their practical support over the years, which has directly affected the amount and quality of my writing.

– Susan McMaster, Ottawa, February 2010

Credits

My sincere thanks to the editors for publications in which these poems have appeared: *A Labour of Love, A Room at the Heart of Things, Anthos, Bookware, Capital Poets, Celebrating Canadian Women, Crossing Boundaries, Full Moon, Line by Line, Living Archives* series, *Next Exit, nth, Other Channels, Passions and Poisons, Poems in Process, Re:Generations, Siolence, The Lunar Plexus, Two Lips, Vintage '93, Waging Peace, Wider Boundaries of Daring, Wild Horse Best Canadian Poems, Women's Art Resource Centre Quilting Project, Seven Poems, Arc, Canadian Author, Carleton Literary Review, Carousel, Event, Graffito, Grain, Los, mother tongues, Oscar, Ottawa Citizen, Poetry Toronto, Poésie Ottawa Poetry, Powder Keg, Quarry, Room of One's Own, Sugar Mule, Toronto Star, Whetstone,* and *Ygdrasil.*

Quotations for poems based on physics are from *Scientific American* 252:5. The phrase "organ music" in "Requiem for organ music" refers to a series of poems on the organs of the body by bpNichol; the title of "Out of the sleeping body dreams erupt" is quoted from his book *The Martyrology: Book 5.* "Prayers in space" is for Bronwen Wallace. "Yeast" is for Penn Kemp. "The naming" is for my daughter Aven McMaster. "For my daughter, in hospital" and "For my daughter, coming home" are for my daughter Morel McMaster. "Choke" is for my late father-in-law, Eric McMaster. Untitled poems headed by the symbol ✦ are from *The Hummingbird Murders.*

The wordmusic poem "Double Vision" that appears, appropriately twice, on the endpapers, offers a taste of my performance work. It is from my first book, *Pass this way again,* co-authored with Andrew McClure and Claude Dupuis, and published by bpNichol through Underwhich Editions in 1983. *Pass* was printed, beautifully, by Stan Bevington at Coach House Press. It is a pleasure to have this selected poems also printed by Coach House almost three decades later.

Sources

The poems in this collection first appeared in the following books.

Dark Galaxies (Ouroboros, 1986)
All her soft angles, Birthday tales, Certain days, Dark matter, Lac Vert, Mail, Pandora, Perceiving a stable environment, Quantum world, Superstring [Spacetime], Supersymmetry, The axion, The letter you do not send, The moth, The need of objects, To admit the draw of starlight, Today I turned everything around, World shift

Dangerous Graces: Women's Poetry on Stage (Balmuir 1987)
Fucking in the afternoon

The Hummingbird Murders (Quarry, 1992)
[original poems were untitled]
Beware, Blame, Dangerous times, Driving into night, Hands in light, It is my own sadness, love is the word, my breath wasn't yours, one handful of bright feathers, Real things, The hummingbird, The logic of hills

Learning to Ride (Quarry, 1994)
As the heart learns to pulse, Daughter, Dismounting, Learning to ride, Mont St-Hilaire, So the mind learns to fly

Uncommon Prayer: A book of dedications (Quarry, 1998)
Beginnings, Choke, Bitter bread, For my daughter, coming home [all is blue], For my daughter, in hospital [Laugh in the face of the devil], Old cedar, Outhouse, How dandelions prey, How God sees, How windows pray, Out of the sleeping body dreams erupt, Pray for me, Prayer for a morning, Recycling, Red, Requiem for organ music, Spacetime quake [part I from Prayers in space], The function of prayer, The gardener's dream, The naming, The pleasure of lusting, The old couch, The old man's chair, The old woman's chair, Prayers in space [part II], Weekend friends, Yeast

Until the Light Bends (Black Moss, 2004)
dream strand: Falling, Door, Ice, Walking the labyrinth – day three: Benign, lately, she remembers: January, lately, she remembers: July, lately, she remembers: March, lately, she remembers: November, Ordinary 1: Ordinary – is it?, Ordinary 5: Confronting it straight, Ordinary 7: She lies so still, Ordinary 8: It is one of the other days, Ordinary 10: Terror of it can't last, Ordinary 11: We can only endure it, Ordinary 12: It comes. The call, Postscript, Starlings, Still enough

New Poems

At midnight, talks fail 1: And here we are, At midnight, talks fail 2: When clouds drift over, At midnight, talks fail 3: An indoor huncher, At midnight, talks fail 4: And still we walk, Black locust fever

For more information on additional publications and recordings by Susan McMaster, please visit http://web.ncf.ca/smcmaster/

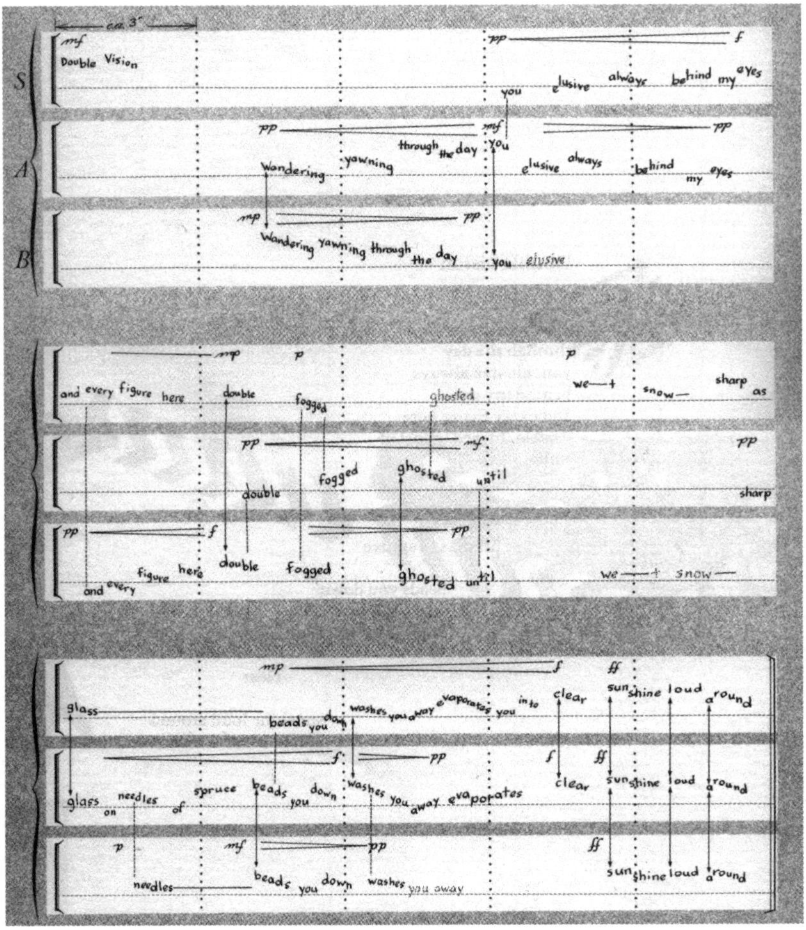

ca. 3"
S
A
B
Double Vision
you elusive always behind my eyes
Wandering yawning through the day you elusive always behind my eyes
Wandering yawning through the day you elusive
and every figure here double fogged ghosted we snow sharp as
double fogged ghosted until sharp
and every figure here double fogged ghosted until we snow
glass beads you down washes you away evaporates you into clear sunshine loud around
glass on needles of spruce beads you down washes you away evaporates clear sunshine loud around
needles beads you down washes you away sunshine loud around